W9-DAU-881

MATH IN OUR WORLD

PIZZA PARTS:
FRACTIONS!

By Linda Bussell

Reading consultant: Susan Nations, M.Ed.,
author/literacy coach/consultant in literacy development
Math consultant: Rhea Stewart, M.A., mathematics content specialist

WEEKLY READER®
PUBLISHING

Please visit our web site at www.garethstevens.com
For a free color catalog describing our list of high-quality books,
call 1-800-542-2595 (USA) or 1-800-387-3178 (Canada). Our fax: 1-877-542-2596

Library of Congress Cataloging-in-Publication Data

Bussell, Linda.
    Pizza parts : fractions! / by Linda Bussell.
        p. cm. — (Math in our world level 3)
    Includes bibliographical references and index.
    ISBN-10: 0-8368-9289-5 — ISBN-13: 978-0-8368-9289-5 (lib. bdg.)
    ISBN-10: 0-8368-9388-3 — ISBN-13: 978-0-8368-9388-5 (softcover)
    1. Fractions—Juvenile literature. I. Title.
    QA117.B92   2009
    513.2'6—dc22   2008010961

This edition first published in 2009 by
Weekly Reader® Books
An Imprint of Gareth Stevens Publishing
1 Reader's Digest Road
Pleasantville, NY 10570-7000 USA

Creative Director: Lisa Donovan
Designer: Amelia Favazza, *Studio Montage*
Copy Editor: Susan Labella
Photo Researcher: Kim Babbitt

Photo Credits: cover, title page: Polka Dot Images/Jupiter Images; pp. 4, 21: David Young-Wolff/Photo Edit; pp. 5, 7, 10, 13, 18, 19: Hemera Technologies; p. 6: Jeff Greenberg/Photo Edit; pp. 8, 9, 11, 12, 13, 14, 17: Russell Pickering

Printed in the United States

1 2 3 4 5 6 7 8 9 10 09 08

Table of Contents

Words that appear in the glossary are printed in **boldface** type the first time they occur in the text.

Chapter 1

Elena's Birthday Plans

Elena is excited! Today is her birthday. She is going to have a party. She is happy to celebrate her special day with friends and family.

Her family owns a pizza parlor. They serve pizza and other food. Elena loves to go there after school. It always smells so good! Her mom and dad both work there. They tell Elena that she can bring her friends to the pizza parlor. She can bring them after school on her birthday.

Elena goes to the pizza parlor with her friends. She is surprised that the restaurant is dark when she first opens the door. Suddenly the room lights up. Her whole family shouts, "Happy Birthday, Elena!"

Elena's family has decorated the restaurant for her birthday. Balloons and streamers hang from the ceiling. There is a giant "Happy Birthday" sign hanging over a big table. Elena's little brother, Dante, says he helped make the sign. Elena gives him a big hug.

Elena's family and friends celebrated her birthday at the pizza parlor.

Chapter 2

Pizza Pieces

Elena smiles as she invites her friends to sit at the big table. She invited 14 friends to her party. Elena's father says they may order any kind of pizza they want. They read their menus. There are so many kinds of pizza it is hard to decide!

Elena and her friends talk about what they want to eat. They decide to order in small groups. That way, they all can have the kind of pizza they want.

Sophia and Priya want a small pizza that is one-**half** cheese and one-half mushroom.

Elena's father writes, "Small pizza, $\frac{1}{2}$ cheese $+ \frac{1}{2}$ mushroom" on his notepad.

He says, "$\frac{1}{2}$ is how we write one-half. The number below the line tells the total number of equal parts the pizza has been divided into. The number above the line tells how many of the equal parts we are talking about."

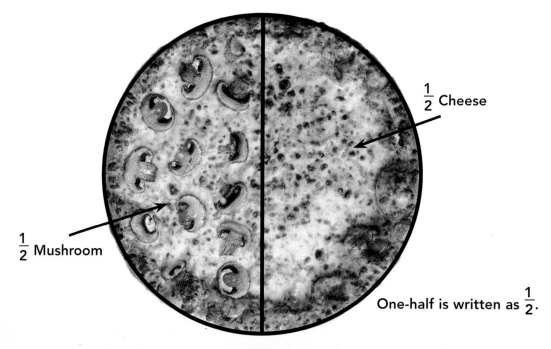

$\frac{1}{2}$ Cheese

$\frac{1}{2}$ Mushroom

One-half is written as $\frac{1}{2}$.

Priya says, "One of two equal parts has mushrooms."

The pizza will be one-half cheese and one-half mushroom.

"Parts of **fractions** have special names," says Sophia.
"The number above the line is called the **numerator**."

Priya adds, "The number below the line is called the
denominator. In the fraction $\frac{1}{2}$, 1 is the numerator, and 2 is
the denominator."

$\frac{1}{2}$	Numerator (number of equal parts we are talking about)
	Denominator (the number of equal parts in the whole)

The top and bottom parts of a fraction have special names.

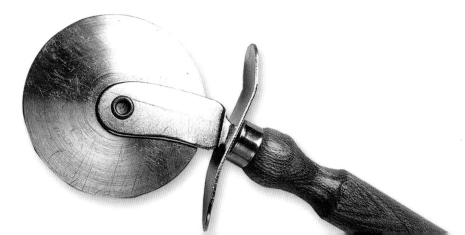

Dylan listens to Priya and Sophia. He asks, "Are you going to eat that whole pizza? I like both cheese and mushrooms on my pizza!"

Priya and Sophia say they will have enough to share with Dylan.

Sophia wonders, "How can we share the pizza so that we each get the same amount?"

"We can use fractions," replies Priya.

Dylan says, "We can divide the pizza into **thirds**. We will each have one-third."

Elena's father says, "$\frac{1}{3}$ is how we write the fraction one-third. It means one part out of three equal parts."

"Sophia and I will have $\frac{2}{3}$ of the pizza," says Priya. "The three of us will have $\frac{3}{3}$ of the pizza!"

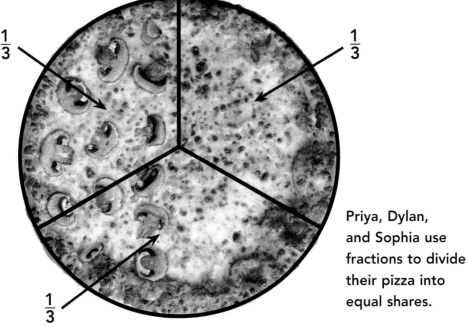

$\frac{1}{3}$

$\frac{1}{3}$

$\frac{1}{3}$

Priya, Dylan, and Sophia use fractions to divide their pizza into equal shares.

11

The next group is ready to order. Eduardo, Kelly, Lexi, and Seth want to share a medium pizza. All of them like vegetables. Seth asks, "How can we share our pizza equally?"

Lexi says, "We can divide the pizza into **fourths**. This means we divide the pizza into four equal parts. One share of the pizza is one-fourth."

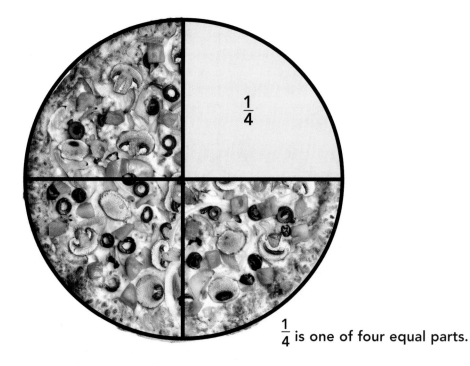

$\frac{1}{4}$ is one of four equal parts.

Four more children place their order. They want to share a large pizza. Elena and Thuy want olives on their pizza. They do not want mushrooms. Melissa and Logan want mushrooms but not olives.

"One-fourth is also written $\frac{1}{4}$. One-fourth means one part out of four equal parts," says Elena's father.

"We will each have one fourth of the vegetable pizza," says Elena.

Melissa asks, "How can we all get what we want?"

Elena says, "We can order a pizza with $\frac{1}{2}$ olives and $\frac{1}{2}$ mushrooms."

"Thuy and I can share the olive half equally," she says. "Melissa and Logan can share the mushroom half equally."

"We each will get the same amount of pizza," says Thuy.

Logan says, "Melissa and I will share $\frac{1}{2}$ of the pizza. The pizza will be cut into fourths. Melissa and I will share $\frac{2}{4}$. We will each have $\frac{1}{4}$ of the pizza!"

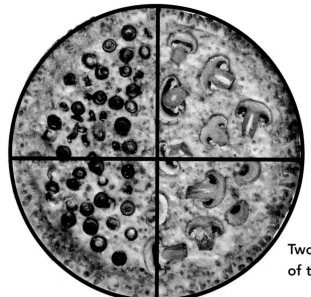

Two people can share $\frac{1}{2}$ of this pizza equally.

Melissa says, "I can see that $\frac{2}{4}$ is the same amount as $\frac{1}{2}$ of the pizza."

Elena's father says, "That's right! I will bring you a pizza with $\frac{1}{2}$ olives and $\frac{1}{2}$ mushrooms. You will each have $\frac{1}{4}$ of the whole pizza."

"We all will get the kind of pizza we want," says Thuy.

The shaded areas are equal.
$\frac{2}{4}$ is the same as $\frac{1}{2}$.

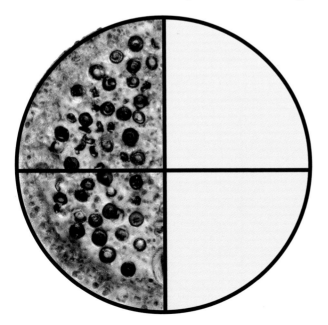 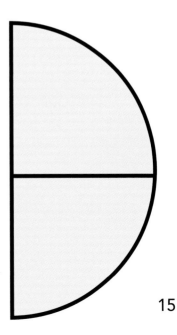

Chapter 3

Smaller Pizza Pieces!

Four other friends want to order some green pepper pizza and some onion pizza.

Evan says, "We can order a pizza that is $\frac{1}{2}$ green pepper and $\frac{1}{2}$ onion. But how can we share it equally?"

Daniela draws a circle on her napkin. She divides the circle in half.

"Now I will divide the circle into four equal parts," she says.

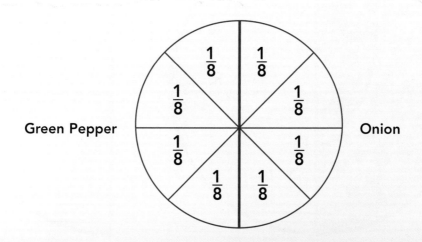

Then she divides the circle again and again. Now the circle is divided into eight equal parts.

Daniela says, "We can divide the pizza into **eighths**, or eight equal parts."

"One piece of the pizza is one-eighth," says Hannah.

Daniela writes $\frac{1}{8}$ on her napkin. "One-eighth means one part of eight equal parts," she says.

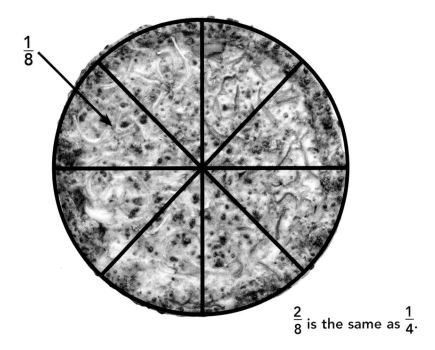

$\frac{1}{8}$

$\frac{2}{8}$ is the same as $\frac{1}{4}$.

"We can cut the pizza into eight equal slices. There will be four slices with green peppers and four slices with onions," says Daniela. "That is enough for each of us to have what we want."

Elena's father takes their order. He will cut their pizza into eighths.

Evan points to Daniela's drawing. He says, "$\frac{2}{8}$ is the same as $\frac{1}{4}$ of the pizza."

Chapter 4

Party Games

Now everyone has ordered pizza. They are ready to eat when Elena's father and mother bring the food to the table. It is quiet while they enjoy the tasty pizza.

Soon everyone is talking again. They ate all the delicious pizza, and they all received the kind of pizza they wanted.

Now, it is time for games, and the 16 friends divide into teams of four. Dante says, "I am $\frac{1}{4}$ of my team." He is right! There are four people on each team. One person is $\frac{1}{4}$ of the whole team.

Elena's father says that fractions are used to name a part of a whole, such as a slice of pizza. Fractions can also name a part of a group, such as one person on a team.

Elena's friends laugh. None of them had ever been called a fraction before!

Next, the friends make new teams to play pretend animals. They will play with two teams. Eight people are on each team. Each person is $\frac{1}{8}$ of a whole team.

They take turns acting like different animals. Soon all the guests are laughing with each other!

Fractions can name a part of a whole.
They also can name a part of a group.

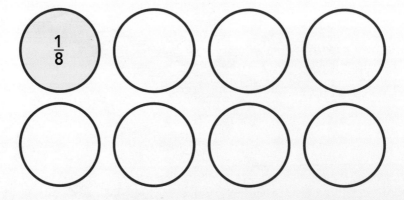

It is almost time for everyone to go home. Elena's friends ask if they may help clean up. They put the pizza pans and dishes on a cart. Elena's father takes the cart to the kitchen. Everything is put away in no time.

Now it is time to say good-bye. Elena has had a great birthday! Her family and friends have had a good time at the celebration.

Elena thanks each guest for coming to her party. The guests thank Elena and her family for a wonderful time.

Elena had a wonderful birthday with her family and friends.

What Did You Learn?

(1) Divide an apple into 3 equal parts. What is the fraction name for each part?

(2) Draw a picture of a pie with 8 pieces in it. Write the fraction name for each piece.

Use a separate piece of paper.

Glossary

denominator: the part of a fraction below the line, which tells how many equal parts there are in the whole or in the group

eighth: one of eight equal parts

fourth: one of four equal parts

fraction: a number that names part of a whole or part of a group

half: one of two equal parts

numerator: the part of a fraction above the line, which tells how many parts are being counted

third: one of three equal parts

Index

About the Author

Linda Bussell has written and designed books, supplemental learning materials, educational games, and software programs for children and young adults. She lives with her family in San Diego, California.